MY FAVORITE WORSHIP SONGS

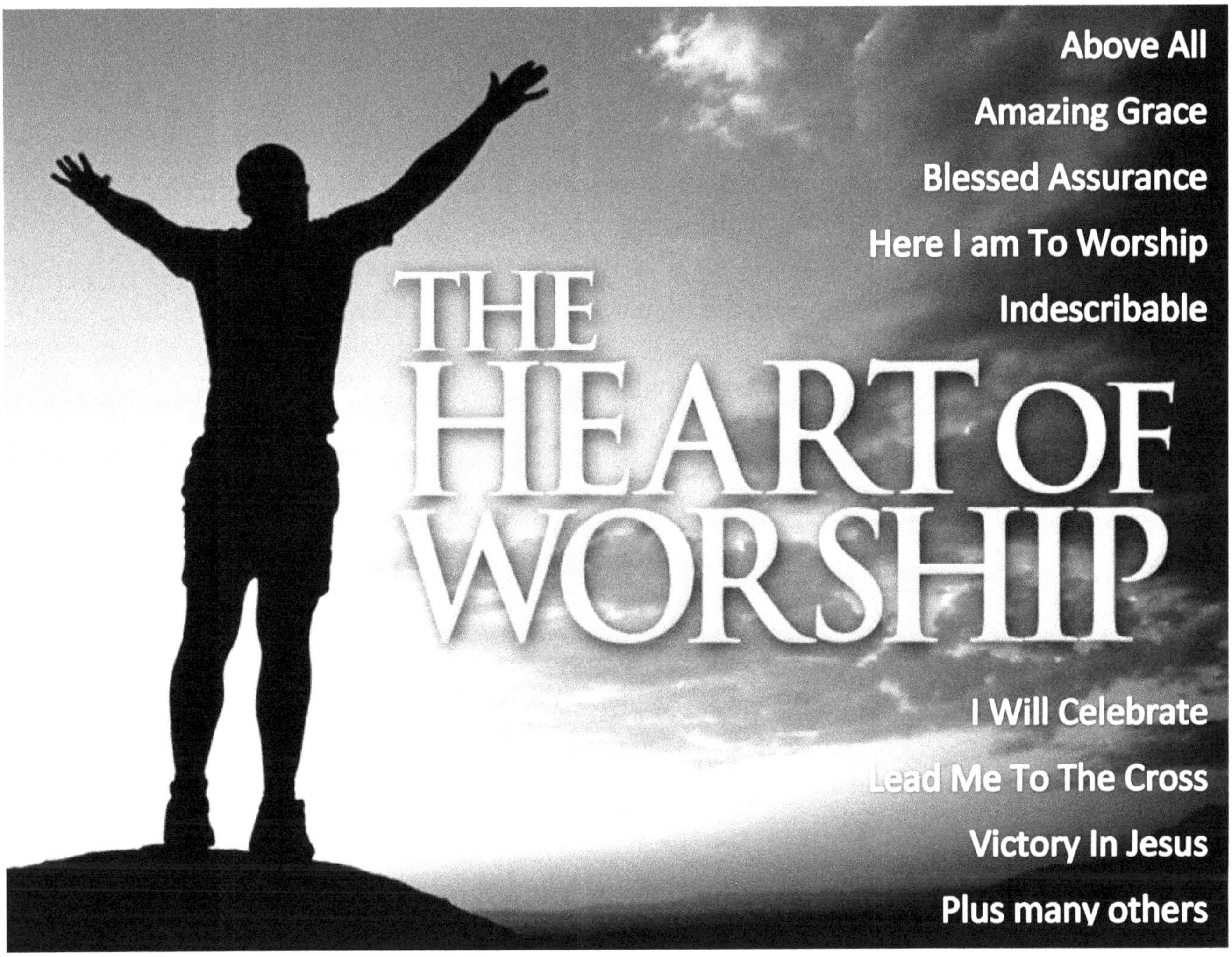

Above All

Amazing Grace

Blessed Assurance

Here I am To Worship

Indescribable

THE HEART OF WORSHIP

I Will Celebrate

Lead Me To The Cross

Victory In Jesus

Plus many others

I will bless the LORD at all times: his praise shall continually be in my mouth. Psalm 34:1

2011

Kevin Airrington

Printed in the United States of America.

ISBN: 978-1-105-11895-1

Published in the United States of America By:

Kevin R Airrington

Airrington Ministries

Emmett, Id 83617

www.airrington.com

email me: kevin@airrington.com

Be sure and order our Christmas Song Book: My Favorite Christmas Songs

Above All

Above all powers, above all kings
Above all nature and all created things
Above all wisdom, and all the ways of man
You were here before the world began

Above all kingdoms, above all thrones
Above all wonders the world has ever known
Above all wealth and treasures of the earth
There's no way to measure what you're worth

Crucified laid behind a stone
You lived to die rejected and alone
Like a rose trampled on the on the ground
You took the fall, and thought of me
Above all

Like a rose
Trampled on the ground
You took the fall
And thought of me
Above all

Alive, Alive

F Bb F C

ALIVE, ALIVE, ALIVE FOREVER MORE. MY JESUS IS

F

ALIVE, ALIVE FOREVER MORE.

F Bb F C

ALIVE, ALIVE, ALIVE FOREVER MORE, MY JESUS IS

F F7

ALIVE, FOREVER MORE.

Bb F C

SING HALLELUJAH, SING HALLELUJAH, MY JESUS

C7 F F7

IS ALIVE FOREVER MORE,

Bb-Bbm F-Dm Gm

SING HALLELUJAH, SING HALLELUJAH, MY JESUS

C F

IS ALIVE

All Day Long

F

ALL DAY LONG I'VE BEEN WITH JESUS,

Bb F

IT HAS BEEN A WONDERFUL DAY

I HAVE CLIMBED UP ONE STEP

G C

HIGHER, IN THAT GOOD OLE FASHION WAY

F

I HAVE SPOKEN WORDS OF KINDNESS

Bb F

LORD YOU KNOW IF I'VE DONE WRONG

I'LL GO OUT AND MAKE IT RIGHT SO

I CAN TESTIFY TONIGHT, I'VE BEEN WITH

C F

JESUS ALL DAY LONG

Amazing Grace

Amazing grace, how sweet the sound
That saved a wretch like me
I once was lost, but now I'm found
Was blind, but now I see.

'Twas grace that taught my heart to fear
And grace that fear relieved
How precious did that grace appear
The hour I first believed.

Through many dangers, toils, and snares, I have already come
'Tis grace has brought me safe thus far
And grace will lead me home.

When we've been there ten thousand years
Bright shining as the sun
We've no less days to sing God's praise
Than when we first begun

How sweet the name of Jesus sounds
In a believer's ear
It soothes his sorrows, heals his wounds
And drives away his fear.

Must Jesus bear the cross alone
And all the world go free
No, there's a cross for everyone
And there's a cross for me.

At The Cross (In F)

F
AT THE CROSS, AT THE CROSS
C
WHERE I FIRST SAW THE LIGHT

AND THE BURDENS OF MY HEART
F F7
ROLLED AWAY,
Bb F Dm
IT WAS THERE BY FAITH, I RECEIVED MY SIGHT,
Gm C F
AND NOW I AM HAPPY ALL THE DAY

At The Cross (In Spanish)(In F)

F C
EN LA CRUZ, EN LA CRUZ, YO PRIMERO VI LA

LUZ
F F7
Y LAS MANCHAS DE MI ALMA EL LAVO
Bb F Dm
FUE ALLI POR FE YO VI A JESUS
Gm C F
Y SIEMPRE FELIZ CON EL SERE

Because He Lives (In F)

```
                F                                  Bb
BECAUSE HE LIVES, I CAN FACE TOMORROW
                   F          G       C    C7
   BECAUSE HE LIVES, ALL FEAR IS GONE
                F   F7               Bb        Bbm
 BECAUSE I KNOW, HE HOLDS THE FUTURE
                         F                   C
AND LIFE IS WORTH THE LIVING JUST BECAUSE
                          F
                      HE LIVES
```

HE SENT HIS SON, THEY CALLED HIM JESUS
HE CAME TO LOVE HEAL AND FORGIVE.
HE LIVED AND DIED TO BUY MY PARDON
AN EMPTY GRAVE IS THERE TO PROVE MY SAVIOR LIVES

HOW SWEET TO HOLD A NEWBORN BABY
AND FEEL THE PRIDE AND JOY HE GIVES
BUT GREATER STILL THE CALM ASSURANCE
THIS CHILD CAN FACE UNCERTAIN DAYS,
BECAUSE HE LIVES

Better Is One Day

How lovely is
Your dwelling place
Oh Lord Almighty,
My soul doth long
And even faint
For You
Here my heart
Is satisfied
Within Your presence
I see beneath
The shadow of
Your wings

Better is one day in Your courts
Better is one day in Your house
Better is one day in Your courts
Than thousands elsewhere
Better is one day in Your courts
Better is one day in Your house
Better is one day in Your courts
Than thousands elsewhere

How lovely is Your dwelling place

Better Is One Day con't

Oh Lord Almighty,
My soul doth long
And even faint
For You
Here my heart
Is satisfied
Within Your presence
I see beneath
The shadow of
Your wings

Better is one day in Your courts
Better is one day in Your house
Better is one day in Your courts
Than thousands elsewhere
Better is one day in Your courts
Better is one day in Your house
Better is one day in Your courts
Than thousands elsewhere

(My heart and flesh cry out)
My heart and flesh cry out
For You, the Living God
Your Spirit's water to my soul
I've tasted, and I've seen, Come once again to me

Better Is One Day con't

I will draw near to You
I will draw near to You
To You

Better is one day in Your courts
Better is one day in Your house
Better is one day in Your courts
Than thousands elsewhere
Better is one day in Your courts
Better is one day in Your house
Better is one day in Your courts
Than thousands elsewhere

Better is one day in Your courts
Better is one day in Your house
Better is one day in Your courts
Than thousands elsewhere
Better is one day in Your courts
Better is one day in Your house
Better is one day in Your courts
Than thousands elsewhere

Bless That Wonderful Name (in G)

BLESS THAT WONDERFUL NAME OF JESUS

BLESS THAT WONDERFUL NAME OF JESUS

BLESS THAT WONDERFUL NAME OF JESUS

NO OTHER NAME I KNOW

THERE'S HEALING IN THE NAME OF JESUS

THERE'S POWER IN THE NAME OF JESUS

Blessed Assurance

Blessed assurance, Jesus is mine!
Oh, what a foretaste of glory divine!
Heir of salvation, purchase of God,
Born of His Spirit, washed in His blood.

Refrain:
This is my story, this is my song,
Praising my Savior all the day long;
This is my story, this is my song,
Praising my Savior all the day long.

Perfect submission, perfect delight,
Visions of rapture now burst on my sight;
Angels, descending, bring from above
Echoes of mercy, whispers of love.

Perfect submission, all is at rest,
I in my Savior am happy and blest,
Watching and waiting, looking above,
Filled with His goodness, lost in His love.

Come Now is the Time to Worship

Come, now is the time to worship
Come, now is the time to give your heart
Come, just as you are to worship
Come, just as you are before your God
Come

(Spoken: One day)
One day ev'ry tongue will confess You are God
One day ev'ry knee will bow
Still the greatest treause remains for those,
Who gladly choose you now

(Spoken: Come)
Come, now is the time to worship
Come, now is the time to give your heart
Come, just as you are to worship
Come, just as you are before your God
Come

(Spoken: One day)
One day ev'ry tongue will confess You are God
One day ev're knee will bow
Still the greates treasure remains for those,
Who gladly choose you now
Ooh, we're calling You
Calling all nations
Now is the time
One day ev'ry tongue will confess You are God
One day ev'ry knee will bow
Still the greatest treasure remains for those,
Who gladly choose you now

(Spoken: One day)
One day ev'ry tongue will confess You are God
One day ev're knee will bow
Still the greates treasure remains for those,
Who gladly choose you now

Come To Jesus

Weak and wounded sinner
Lost and left to die
O, raise your head, for love is passing by
Come to Jesus
Come to Jesus
Come to Jesus and live!

Now your burden's lifted
And carried far away
And precious blood has washed away the stain, so
Sing to Jesus
Sing to Jesus
Sing to Jesus and live!

And like a newborn baby
Don't be afraid to crawl
And remember when you walk
Sometimes we fall...so
Fall on Jesus
Fall on Jesus
Fall on Jesus and live!

Sometimes the way is lonely
And steep and filled with pain
So if your sky is dark and pours the rain, then
Cry to Jesus
Cry to Jesus, Cry to Jesus and live!

Come To Jesus con't

O, and when the love spills over
And music fills the night
And when you can't contain your joy inside, then
Dance for Jesus
Dance for Jesus
Dance for Jesus and live!

And with your final heartbeat
Kiss the world goodbye
Then go in peace, and laugh on Glory's side, and
Fly to Jesus
Fly to Jesus
Fly to Jesus and live!

C’mon and Praise the Lord (in F)

```
                    F
C’mon and Praise the Lord, Praise the Lord
                    C
Let all God’s children praise the Lord
          F                   Bb
Shake off those heavy bands; lift up those holy hands
          F          C          F
Let all God’s children praise the Lord
```

Create In Me A Clean Heart (in G)

```
      G          Bm       C      G
CREATE IN ME A CLEAN HEART, OH GOD
               D           G
AND RENEW A RIGHT SPIRIT WITHIN ME ( 2X)

        C          D               G
CAST ME NOT AWAY FROM YOUR PRESENCE OH
                  Em
                 LORD
      C          D               G
TAKE NOT THY HOLY SPIRIT FROM ME
           C         D      G
RESTORE UNTO ME, THE JOY OF THY
                  Em
              SALVATION
      C                D            G
AND RENEW A RIGHT SPIRIT WITHIN ME
```

Days of Elijah

These are the days of Elijah...declaring the word of the Lord

These are the days of your servant Moses,
Righteousness being restored

And though these are the days of great trials, of famine and darkness and sore

Still we are the voice in the desert crying, "Prepare ye the way of the Lord."

Behold he comes riding on the clouds shining like the sun
at the Trumpets call
Lift your voice it's the year of jubilee
Out of Zion's hills salvation comes

These are the days of Ezekiel, the dry bones becoming as flesh
These are the days of your servant David, rebuilding a temple of praise
And these are the days of the harvest the fields are as white in your world
And we are the laborers in your vineyard declaring the word of the Lord

There's no God like Jehovah (repeat)......

God's Got An Army (in E)

E
GOD'S GOT AN ARMY MARCHING THROUGH THE LAND
B
DELIVERANCE IS THEIR SONG
E
WITH HEALING IN THEIR HAND
C#m7
EVER LASTING JOY AND GLADNESS IN THEIR HEARTS
A B E
AND IN THIS ARMY I'VE GOT A PART
E7
WITH THE HIGH PRAISES OF GOD IN THEIR HEARTS
A E
AND A TWO EDGED SWORD IN THEIR HAND
C#m
WE WILL MARCH RIGHT UP TO THE VICTORY SIDE,
A B E
RIGHT INTO CANAAN'S LAND

SINGING LET THE OPPRESSED GO FREE,
B
LET THE OPPRESSED GO FREE
E E7 A
THERE'S DELIVERANCE AND POWER FOR YOU AND ME,
E B E
LET THE OPPRESSED GO FREE

God of Wonders

Lord of all creation
of water earth and sky
The heavens are your Tabernacle
Glory to the Lord on high

Chorus:
God of wonders beyond our galaxy
You are Holy, Holy
The universe declares your Majesty
And you are holy holy

Lord of Heaven and Earth
Lord of Heaven and Earth

Early in the morning
I will celebrate the light
When I stumble in the darkness
I will call your name by night

chrous
Lord of heaven and earth
Lord of heaven and earth

Hallelujah to the Lord of heaven and earth (repeat 3 times)

holy......holy....holy God.....

Chorus

Precious Lord reveal your love to me....
Father holy...
(Background)...Lord God almighty...

The "universe" declares your majesty
"you are" holy,holy,holy,holy
Halleujah to the Lord of heaven and earth 9x

Hallelujah (Your love is amazing) (in G)

G/B C2
Your love is amazing, steady and unchanging
Dsus C2
Your love is a mountain, firm beneath my feet
G/B C2
Your love is a mystery, how you gently lift me
Dsus C2
When I am surrounded, your love carries me

G/B C2
Your love is surprising, I can feel it rising
Dsus C2
All the joy that's growing, deep inside of me
G/B C2
Every time I praise you, I know that I please you
Dsus C2
And I can sense your presence, rising up in me

G Dsus Em7
Hallelujah, hallelujah, hallelujah
C2
Your love makes me sing (2x)

Here I Am To Worship

Light of the world
You stepped down into darkness
Opened my eyes let me see
Beauty that made this heart adore You
Hope of a life spent with You

Here I am to worship
Here I am to bow down
Here I am to say that You're my God
You're altogether lovely
Altogether worthy
Altogether wonderful to me

King of all days
O so highly exalted
Glorious in Heaven above
Humbly You came to the earth You created
All for love's sake became poor

I'll never know how much it cost
To see my sin upon the cross

...Worship You
Hallelujah, Hallelujah
I worship You for who You are

I worship You
Hallelujah, Hallelujah
I worship You for who You are

Holy of Holies

(In Em # 1 OF 1 SLOW)

```
                    Em                                        C
TAKE ME PAST THE OUTER COURTS, INTO YOUR
                                        D
HOLY PLACE PAST THE BRAZEN ALTAR LORD I
                 Em                    D                 Em
WANT TO SEE YOU FACE--PASS ME BY THE
                                    C
CROWDS OF PEOPLE, THE PRIESTS WHO SING
                                         D
YOUR PRAISE, I HUNGER AND I THIRST FOR YOUR
                                      Am
RIGHTEOUSNESS, AND IT'S ONLY FOUND IN ONE
                                         D
PLACE
                     Em                          D
TAKE ME INTO THE HOLY OF HOLIES, TAKE ME
       Am                G                   Em  C^D                 Em
IN BY THE BLOOD OF THE LAMB TAKE ME INTO
                           D                             C
THE HOLY OF HOLIES, TAKE THE COAL, CLEANSE
                 Bm               C MAJ7                    Am
MY LIPS HERE I AM      TAKE THE COAL CLEANSE
                          D                  Em
MY LIPS HERE I AM
```

Indescribable

Indescribable, uncontainable
You placed the stars in the sky
And You know them by name
You are amazing God

All powerful, untamable
Awestruck we fall to our knees
As we humbly proclaim
You are amazing God

Indescribable, uncontainable
You placed the stars in the sky
And You know them by name
You are amazing, God

Incomparable, unchangeable
You see the depths of my heart
And You love me the same
You are amazing, God
You are amazing, God

I Command You Satan (in F)

```
                                F
I command you Satan in the Name of the Lord
                          C
          To pick up your weapons and flee
               F              Bb          F          C   F
For the Lord has given authority to stomp all over thee
```

I Exalt Thee (in E)

E F#m
FOR THOU, O LORD
B7 E B C#m
ART HIGH ABOVE ALL THE EARTH
F#m B7 Bsus E
THOU ARE EXALTED FAR ABOVE ALL GODS.
F# A/B
FOR THOU O LORD ART HIGH
E G#7 C#m
ABOVE ALL THE EARTH
F#m B7 E
THOU ART EXALTED FAR ABOVE ALL GODS.

A/B B7 E B/D#
I EXALT THEE, I EXALT THEE
A add2 A A/B B7 E B7
I EXALT THEE, O LORD
E B/D#
I EXALT THEE, I EXALT THEE
A add2 A B7 E
I EXALT THEE O LORD

In Christ Alone

In Christ alone my hope is found
He is my light, my strength, my song
This Cornerstone, this solid ground
Firm through the fiercest drought and storm
What heights of love, what depths of peace
When fears are stilled, when strivings cease
My Comforter, my All in All
Here in the love of Christ I stand

In Christ alone, who took on flesh
Fullness of God in helpless babe
This gift of love and righteousness
Scorned by the ones He came to save
'Til on that cross as Jesus died
The wrath of God was satisfied
For every sin on Him was laid
Here in the death of Christ I live

There in the ground His body lay
Light of the world by darkness slain
Then bursting forth in glorious Day
Up from the grave He rose again
And as He stands in victory
Sin's curse has lost its grip on me
For I am His and He is mine
Bought with the precious blood of Christ

No guilt of life, no fear in death
This is the power of Christ in me
From life's first cry to final breath
Jesus commands my destiny
No power of hell, no scheme of man
Can ever pluck me from His hand
'til He returns or calls me home
Here in the power of Christ I'll stand

I want You To Know

In the secret, in the quiet place
In the stillness You are there
In the secret, in the quiet hour
I wait only for You
Cause, I want to know You more

I want to know You
I want to hear Your voice
I want to know You more
I want to touch You
I want to see Your face
I want to know You more

I am reaching for the highest goal
That I might receive the prize
Pressing onward, pushing every hindrance aside
Out of my way
Cause, I want to know You more

I Will Celebrate

SING UNTO THE LORD

I WILL SING TO HIM A NEW SONG

(REPEAT)

I WILL PRAISE HIM

I WILL SING TO HIS A NEW SONG

I WILL PRAISE HIM

I WILL SING TO HIS A NEW SONG

HALLELUJAH, HALLELUJAH

HAL-LE-LU, HALLELUJAH

I will enter In his Gates (in G)

G D C
I will enter in His gates,
D G D C
with thanksgiving in my heart
D G D C
I will enter in His courts...
D
with praise
G D C
I will say this is the day
D G D C
that the Lord has made.
C D G
I will rejoice for He has made me glad.

G C
He has made me glad,
G Em
he has made me glad
C D G
I will rejoice for he has made me glad

I will Rise

There's a peace I've come to know
Though my heart and flesh may fail
There's an anchor for my soul
I can say "It is well"

Jesus has overcome
And the grave is overwhelmed
The victory is won
He is risen from the dead

[Chorus:]
And I will rise when He calls my name
No more sorrow, no more pain
I will rise on eagles' wings
Before my God fall on my knees
And rise
I will rise

There's a day that's drawing near
When this darkness breaks to light
And the shadows disappear
And my faith shall be my eyes

Jesus has overcome

I Will Rise (Con't)

And the grave is overwhelmed
The victory is won
He is risen from the dead

[Chorus:]
And I will rise when He calls my name
No more sorrow, no more pain
I will rise on eagles' wings
Before my God fall on my knees
And rise
I will rise

And I hear the voice of many angels sing,
"Worthy is the Lamb"
And I hear the cry of every longing heart,
"Worthy is the Lamb"
[x2]

[Chorus:]
And I will rise when He calls my name
No more sorrow, no more pain
I will rise on eagles' wings
Before my God fall on my knees
And rise
I will rise

I'm So Glad That The Lord Saved Me (in G)

G C G
I'm so glad that the Lord saved me

A D
I'm so glad that the Lord saved me

G G7
If it had not been for Jesus,
C
where would I be?
G D
I'm so glad that the Lord saved me

I've got my mind made up to serve the Lord (in G)

G
I've got my mind made up to serve the Lord
A D
I've got my mind made up to serve the Lord
G G7 C
I've got my mind made up to serve the Lord

G D G
Lord I've got my mind made up
To praise his name
To stay on fire

Jehovah Jirah (in Em)

Em
JEHOVAH JIREH
Am Em
MY PROVIDER HIS GRACE IS
D Em
SUFFICIENT FOR ME FOR ME FOR ME
Em
JEHOVAH JIREH
Am Em
MY PROVIDER HIS GRACE IS
D Em
SUFFICIENT FOR ME

Em Am
MY GOD SHALL SUPPLY ALL YOUR NEEDS
D Em B7
ACCORDING TO HIS RICHES IN GLORY
Am
HE SHALL GIVE HIS ANGELS CHARGE OVER THEE
C D Em
JEHOVAH JIREH CARES FOR ME FOR ME FOR ME
C D Em
JEHOVAH JIREH CARES FOR ME

Jesus Lover of My Soul (in G)

```
            G        D
      JESUS LOVER OF MY SOUL
          Em              C
   JESUS I WILL NEVER LET YOU GO
           G                     D
YOU'VE TAKEN ME FROM THE MIRY CLAY
        Em                          C
SET MY FEET UPON THE ROCK…. NOW I KNOW
```

```
            G              D
       I LOVE YOU, I NEED YOU
        Em                           C
YOU'RE MY ONLY HOPE I'LL NEVER LET YOU GO
         G               D                Em
     MY SAVIOR, MY CLOSEST FRIEND
                      C
 I WILL WORSHIP YOU UNTIL THE VERY END
```

John Was In The Spirit (in G)

```
                  G                                      G7
John was in the spirit on the Lord's day
                 C                                               G
He heard a voice from heaven and this is what it said
                                            Em
I'm the Alpha, Omega, Beginning, and the End,
               C      D          G
Behold I live forever more
```

```
            G                  G7
Behold I live, behold I live
               C            G
Behold I live forever more
                       Em
Behold I live behold I live
               G      D          G
Behold I live forevermore
```

Lord I Lift Your Name On High (in Ab)

Ab Db Eb Db Eb
LORD I LIFT YOUR NAME ON HIGH
Ab Db Eb Db Eb
LORD I LOVE TO SING YOU PRAISES
Ab Db Eb Db Eb
I'M SO GLAD YOU'RE IN MY LIFE
Ab Db Eb Db Eb
I'M SO GLAD YOU CAME TO SAVE US

Ab Db Eb
YOU CAME FROM HEAVEN TO EARTH
Db Eb Ab
TO SHOW THE WAY
Db Eb
FROM THE EARTH TO THE CROSS
Db Eb Ab Db Eb
MY DEBT TO PAY FROM THE CROSS TO THE GRAVE
Fm7 Bbm7
FROM THE GRAVE TO THE SKY
Ebsus Eb Ab
LORD I LIFT YOUR NAME ON HIGH

Majesty (in G)

G C Am
MAJESTY, WORSHIP HIS MAJESTY
G Em Am D
UNTO JESUS BE ALL GLORY, HONOR AND PRAISE
G C Am
MAJESTY, KINGDOM AUTHORITY,
G
FLOWS FROM HIS THRONE
D7 G
UNTO HIS OWN...HIS ANTHEM RAISE

D D7 C G
SO EXALT LIFT UP ON HIGH THE NAME OF JESUS
D D7 G C D7
MAGNIFY, COME GLORIFY CHRIST JESUS THE KING
G G7 C Am
MAJESTY, WORSHIP HIS MAJESTY
G/D D7
JESUS WHO DIED NOW GLORIFIED,
G
KING OF ALL KINGS!

Mary Did You Know

Mary, did you know
that your Baby Boy would one day walk on water?
Mary, did you know
that your Baby Boy would save our sons and daughters?
Did you know
that your Baby Boy has come to make you new?
This Child that you delivered will soon deliver you.

Mary, did you know
that your Baby Boy will give sight to a blind man?
Mary, did you know
that your Baby Boy will calm the storm with His hand?
Did you know
that your Baby Boy has walked where angels trod?
When you kiss your little Baby you kissed the face of God?

Mary did you know.. Ooo Ooo Ooo

The blind will see.
The deaf will hear.
The dead will live again.
The lame will leap.
The dumb will speak
The praises of The Lamb.

Mary, did you know
that your Baby Boy is Lord of all creation?
Mary, did you know
that your Baby Boy would one day rule the nations?
Did you know
that your Baby Boy is heaven's perfect Lamb?
The sleeping Child you're holding is the Great, I Am.

Mighty To Save

Everyone needs compassion
A love that's never failing
Let mercy fall on me
Everyone needs forgiveness
A kindness of a Savior
The hope of nations

Savior
He can move the mountains
My God is Mighty to save
He is Mighty to save
Forever
Author of salvation
He rose and conquered the grave
Jesus conquered the grave

So take me as You find me
All my fears and failures
Fill my life again
I give my life to follow
Everything I believe in
Now I surrender
Yes I surrender
Savior

Mighty To Save Con't

He can move the mountains
My God is Mighty to save
He is Mighty to save
Forever
Author of salvation
He rose and conquered the grave
Jesus conquered the grave

Shine your light and let the whole world see
We're singing for the glory of the risen King...Jesus (x2)

Savior
He can move the mountains
My God is Mighty to save
He is Mighty to save
Forever
Author of salvation
He rose and conquered the grave
Jesus conquered the grave

More Love, More Power

```
      Em                           C           D          Bm
MORE LOVE, MORE POWER, MORE OF YOU IN MY
                            Em    C  D
                          LIFE
        Em              C                D          Bm
MORE LOVE, MORE POWER, MORE OF YOU IN MY
                               Em
                          LIFE

Em                          D            Bm                         Em
   I WILL WORSHIP YOU WITH ALL OF MY HEART
                      D                  Bm                     Em
   I WILL WORSHIP YOU WITH ALL OF MY MIND
                       D                 Bm                     Em
 I WILL WORSHIP YOU WITH ALL OF MY STRENGTH
                           C-D               Em
    FOR YOU ARE MY LORD, YOU ARE MY GOD
```

Our God Reigns (in Bb)

```
Bb                  Eb          F                                          Eb
    HOW LOVELY ON THE MOUNTAINS ARE THE FEET
Bb                                              Cm     F              Bb  Bb7
    OF HIM THAT BRINGS GOOD NEWS, GOOD NEWS
                                         Eb                 F
     ANNOUNCING PEACE, PROCLAIMING NEWS OF
                                   Eb  Bb
                            HAPPINESS,

                              Cm     F                    Bb
           OUR GOD REIGNS, OUR GOD REIGNS,

                              Eb                          Bb
           OUR GOD REIGNS, OUR GOD REIGNS,
                            Eb     F               Bb
           OUR GOD REIGNS, OUR GOD REIGNS
```

Shine Jesus Shine (in G)

```
        G           C                 G          D
LORD THE LIGHT OF YOUR LOVE IS SHINING
      G       C               G            D
IN THE MIDST OF THE DARKNESS SHINING
      C         D              Bm          Em
JESUS, LIGHT OF THE WORLD, SHINE UPON
      C         D             Bm                Em
SET US FREE BY THE TRUTH YOU NOW BRING US,
          F         D     F         D
SHINE ON ME, SHINE ON ME.

        G      D/G G   C
SHINE JESUS SHINE
      G/B    Am                  Dsus        D
FILL THIS LAND WITH THE FATHER'S GLORY
        G      D/G G    C
BLAZE SPIRIT BLAZE
   G/B        Am          F        Dsus  D
SET OUR HEARTS ON FIRE
        G      D/G G    C
FLOW RIVER, FLOW
   G/B         Am                Dsus             D
FLOOD THE NATIONS WITH GRACE AND MERCY
         G     D/G       G     C
SEND FORTH YOUR WORD
         G/B      Am   D7         G
LORD AND LET THERE BE LIGHT
```

The Old Rugged Cross

On a hill far away stood an old rugged cross,
The emblem of suff'ring and shame;
And I love that old cross where the dearest and best
For a world of lost sinners was slain.

Refrain:
So I'll cherish the old rugged cross,
Till my trophies at last I lay down;
I will cling to the old rugged cross,
And exchange it some day for a crown.

Oh, that old rugged cross, so despised by the world,
Has a wondrous attraction for me;
For the dear Lamb of God left His glory above
To bear it to dark Calvary.

In that old rugged cross, stained with blood so divine,
A wondrous beauty I see,
For 'twas on that old cross Jesus suffered and died,
To pardon and sanctify me.

To the old rugged cross I will ever be true;
Its shame and reproach gladly bear;
Then He'll call me some day to my home far away,
Where His glory forever I'll share.

The Spirit of David (in Am)

Am E7
WHEN THE SPIRIT OF THE LORD MOVES UPON
E7 Am (AGAE)
MY HEART I WILL DANCE LIKE DAVID DANCED

Am E7
WHEN THE SPIRIT OF THE LORD MOVES UPON
E7 Am A7
MY HEART I WILL DANCE LIKE DAVID DANCED

Dm G C maj7 F Bm
I WILL DANCE, DANCE, DANCE
E Am A7
LIKE DAVID DANCED
Dm G Cmaj F Bm
I WILL DANCE, DANCE, DANCE
E Am (AGAE)
LIKE DAVID DANCED

I WILL PRAISE...

I WILL SING...

Trading my Sorrows

I'm trading my sorrow
I'm trading my shame
I'm laying it down for the joy of the Lord

I'm trading my sickness
I'm trading my pain
I'm laying it down for the joy of the Lord

Chorus:
And we say yes Lord yes Lord yes yes Lord
Yes Lord yes Lord yes yes Lord
Yes Lord yes Lord yes yes Lord Amen

I'm pressed but not crushed persecuted not abandoned
Struck down but not destroyed
I'm blessed beyond the curse for his promise will endure
And his joy's gonna be my strength

Though the sorrow may last for the night
His joy comes with the morning

Strong Tower

When I wander through the desert
And I'm longing for my home
All my dreams have gone astray
When I'm stranded in the valley
And I'm tired and all alone
It seems like I've lost my way

I go running to your mountain
Where your mercy sets me free

[chorus]
You are my strong tower
Shelter over me
Beautiful and mighty
Everlasting King
You are my strong tower
Fortress when I'm weak
Your name is true and holy
And Your face is all I seek

Strong Tower Con't

In the middle of my darkness

In the midst of all my fear

You're my refuge and my hope

When the storm of life is raging

And the thunder's all I hear

You speak softly to my soul

Lead Me To The Cross

Savior i come, quiet my soul

remember. redemption's hill,

where your blood was spilled

for my ransom

(bridge)

everything i once held dear

i count it all as lost

(chorus)

lead me to the cross,

where your love poured out.

bring me to my knees

lord, i lay me down.

rid me of myself i belong to you,

and lead me, lead me, lead me to the cross.

(verse 2)

you were as i, tempted and trialed

you are, word became flesh

bore my sin and death

now you're risen

to your heart

to your heart

lead me to your heart

to your heart

Power In The Blood (in G)

There is power, power wonder working Power
in the blood of the Lamb
There is power, power wonder working Power
in the precious blood of the Lamb

Would you be free from your burden of sin?
There's power in the blood, power in the Blood,
Would you over evil a victory win?
There's wonderful power in the blood

Would you be free from your passion and pride?
There's power in the blood, Power in the blood,
come for a cleansing to Calvary's tide.
There's wonderful power in the blood

Would you be whiter much whiter Than snow
there's power in the blood, Power in the blood,
sin stains are lost in its life-giving flow
There's wonderful power in the blood

Would you do service for Jesus your King?
There's power in the blood, power In the blood,
would you live daily his Praises to sing?
There's wonderful power in the blood

This is my Desire (in G)

```
      G             Em         C  G   D
THIS IS MY DESIRE, TO HONOR YOU
   Em                    G                  F  D
LORD WITH ALL MY HEART I WORSHIP YOU
     G              Em            C    G    D
ALL I HAVE WITHIN ME, I GIVE YOU PRAISE
     Em           G        F  D
ALL THAT I ADORE IS IN YOU

     G                     D
LORD I GIVE YOU MY HEART
          Am7
I GIVE YOU MY SOUL
     C          D    G
I LIVE FOR YOU ALONE
          D
EVERY BREATH THAT I TAKE
          Am7
EVERY MOMENT I'M AWAKE
     C           D       G
LORD HAVE YOUR WAY IN ME
```

This Is the Day in (in F)

F
This is the day, this is the day

C F
That the Lord has made, that the Lord has made

C
I will rejoice, I will rejoice and be glad in it

F
and be glad in it.

Bb F
This is day that the Lord has made,

Bb F
I will rejoice and be glad in it

C
This is the day, this is the day that the Lord has made

Turn Your Eyes Upon Jesus

O soul, are you weary and troubled?
No light in the darkness you see?
There's light for a look at the Savior,
And life more abundant and free!

Refrain:
Turn your eyes upon Jesus,
Look full in His wonderful face,
And the things of earth will grow strangely dim,
In the light of His glory and grace.

Through death into life everlasting
He passed, and we follow Him there;
O'er us sin no more hath dominion—
For more than conqu'rors we are!

His Word shall not fail you—He promised;
Believe Him, and all will be well:
Then go to a world that is dying,
His perfect salvation to tell!

Victory In Jesus (in G)

Oh victory in Jesus my savior forever
He sought me and bought me with his redeeming blood
He loved me 'ere I knew him and all my love is due him, he plunged me to victory beneath the
Cleansing flood.

I heard an old, old story how a savior came from glory
How he gave his life On Calvary to save a wretch like me
I heard about his groaning, of his precious blood's atoning then I repented of my sins and won the victory

I heard about his healing
Of his cleansing power revealing
How he made the lame to walk again
And caused the blind to see
And then I cried dear Jesus
Come and heal my broken spirit
And somehow Jesus came and brought to me
The victory

I heard about a mansion
He has built for me in glory
And I heard about the streets of gold
Beyond the crystal sea
About the angels singing,
And the old redemption story,
And some sweet day
I'll sing up there the song of victory

www.ingramcontent.com/pod-product-compliance
Ingram Content Group UK Ltd.
Pitfield, Milton Keynes, MK11 3LW, UK
UKHW051135260726
13967UKWH00010B/3066